# FEEL THE G's

## The Science of **Gravity and G-Forces**

by Suzanne Slade

Content Adviser:
Leland Stone, Ph.D.,
NASA, Human Systems Integration Division

Science Adviser:
Terrence E. Young Jr., M.Ed., M.L.S.,
Jefferson Parish (Louisiana) Public School System

Reading Adviser:
Rosemary G. Palmer, Ph.D., Department of Literacy,
College of Education, Boise State University

Compass Point Books • 151 Good Counsel Drive, P.O. Box 669 • Mankato, MN 56002-0669


Printed in the United States of America.

This book was manufactured with paper containing at least 10 percent post-consumer waste.

**Library of Congress Cataloging-in-Publication Data**
Slade, Suzanne.
Feel the G's : the science of gravity and G-forces / by Suzanne Slade.
p. cm.—(Headline Science)
Includes bibliographical references and index.
ISBN 978-0-7565-4052-4 (library binding)
1. Gravity—Juvenile literature. 2. Force and energy—Juvenile literature. I. Title.
QC178.S493 2009
531'.14—dc22 2008038376

Editor: Anthony Wacholtz
Designers: Ellen Schofield and Ashlee Suker
Page Production: Ashlee Suker
Photo Researcher: Eric Gohl

Art Director: LuAnn Ascheman-Adams
Creative Director: Joe Ewest
Editorial Director: Nick Healy
Managing Editor: Catherine Neitge

Photographs ©: AP Images/David J. Phillip, cover (bottom); NASA/Scott Andrews, cover (inset, left), 15; Kevin Tavares/Shutterstock, cover (inset, middle), 9; Arvind Balaraman/Shutterstock, cover (inset, right), 27; Stan Honda/AFP/Getty Images, 5; Chad Slattery/Stone/Getty Images, 7; Candy Hood/Shutterstock, 8; TommL/iStockphoto, 11; NASA/George Shelton, 13; NASA, 16, 28, 29; Check Six/Getty Images, 18; Gavin Lawrence/Getty Images, 21; AP Images/David Kohl, 22; AP Images/*Sandusky Register*, Tim Fleck, 23; Steve Broer/Shutterstock, 25; Graham Heywood/iStockphoto, 26; Jimmy Cribb/AFL via Getty Images, 31; James M Phelps, Jr./Shutterstock, 32; DVIC/SSgt Cherie A. Thurlby, USAF, 33; Cordelia Molloy/Photo Researchers, Inc, 34 (all); AP Images/Carolyn Kaster, 36; AP Images/Texas Motor Speedway, Brian Lawdermilk, 37; Francis Miller/Time Life Pictures/Getty Images, 38; Hulton Archive/Getty Images, 40; Keystone/Getty Images, 41; AP Images/*Alamogordo Daily News*, Ellis Neel, 42; AP Images/Charles Rex Arbogast, 43.

Visit Compass Point Books on the Internet at *www.compasspointbooks.com*
or e-mail your request to *custserv@compasspointbooks.com*

# MATCHUP OF MAN VS. MACHINE: REBEL REPORTER SLAYS KINGDA KA IN DEBUT RUN

*The Trentonian*
May 20, 2005

Strapped in tightly, some say their prayers; others covered their eyes and the brave lifted their arms up in victory as they awaited that fateful sound of the launch buzzer which revs the heavy-lifting hydraulics, giving the rider a clear view of the impending terror that awaits. ...

WOOOOOSHHHH ... a G-force launch wraps your skin around the back of your seat, making you feel like you're leaving your cheeks back at the station.

The pressure forces your eyes, in which your eyelids start to flutter, to smack back into the sockets of your skull, as the sled shoots straight up into the atmosphere.

When the tallest and fastest roller coaster on Earth opened in 2005, people around the world flocked to Six Flags Great Adventure in New Jersey. Hundreds of roller coaster fans stood in long lines for an exhilarating ride on Kingda Ka. After finally arriving at the front of the line, eager passengers fastened their belts tightly for the ride of their lives.

Roller coasters often start off slowly and gently, but this $25 million ride begins by catapulting its passengers from 0 to 128 miles (206 kilometers) per hour in only 3.5 seconds. This incredible acceleration smashes riders back into their seats, giving them a small taste of Kingda Ka's unbelievable power. Then riders brace themselves for the daring drop ahead as they are slowly carried up a 456-foot (139-meter) steel tower. When the chain of cars starts to plummet down the spiraling track, many close their eyes and grip the bar in front of them. Others hold their hands high in the air. Stomachs lurch and churn. Riders scream with fear and delight.

*At its highest point, Kingda Ka is 36 feet (11 m) taller than the next closest roller coaster.*

These high-speed thrills and chills are mostly due to g-force.

## THE MYSTERY OF G-FORCE

Lots of people love roller coasters. They enjoy the sensations they feel

## KEEPING CURRENT

News changes every minute, and readers need access to the latest information to keep current. Here are a few key search terms to help you locate up-to-the-minute gravity and g-forces headlines:

accelerometer measure g-force

antigravity suit (or g-suit)

Air Force Aerospace Medical Research Lab g-force

astronaut or pilot g-force training

fighter pilot sustained g-force

g-induced loss of consciousness (g-LOC)

NASA g-force research testing

roller coaster g-forces

with every upward loop, downward drop, and sideways curve. Hurtling over steel track, riders are pushed back, pulled forward, and sometimes feel as if they are floating. These "pushing," "pulling," and "weightless" sensations are caused by g-force. Whenever you change speed or direction, g-force affects your body. The greater the g-force, the more impact it has on a person. So what exactly is g-force? Some say it is the force that makes roller coasters exciting, but

## NOW YOU KNOW

Most roller coasters are designed to create a maximum 3.5 g's. However, the Aerosmith Rock 'n' Roller Coaster at Walt Disney World in Orlando, Florida, creates an impressive 5 g's when it goes from 0 to 57 miles (92 km) per hour in only 2.8 seconds!

*During a roller coaster ride, the amount of g-forces a person feels increases during the curves in the track.*

scientists define g-force as the force of gravity or acceleration on a body.

## IT'S ALL ABOUT ACCELERATION

The term g-force refers to the force acting upon a person's body as he or she accelerates. Although most people think of an object gaining speed when they think of acceleration, there are three ways acceleration occurs. One type of acceleration is when an object speeds up, such as a race car that suddenly takes off from a starting line. This kind of acceleration creates a g-force that pushes the driver back into his or her seat.

Another type of acceleration occurs when an object slows down. This is called deceleration. If a race car hits the wall surrounding the track, the driver will lurch forward and experience a powerful g-force that is due to the instant reduction in speed.

Acceleration is also created by a change in direction. Race car drivers slow down when they approach a curve in the track because they know the upcoming change in direction will cause acceleration and an increase in g-force. Skilled drivers slow down while going through a sharp curve to keep control of their car and prevent high g-forces.

## THE "G" IN G-FORCE

How did scientists come up with the name *g-force*? The answer lies with the first letter of this word: g.

Earth's gravity pulls objects toward it. When a baseball player hits a homerun, gravity eventually brings the ball back to the ground. Gravity pulls water down a mountain and creates magnificent waterfalls. Gravity also affects how much an object weighs, or how heavy it feels.

*Race car drivers must make gradual turns on the race track to avoid high g-forces.*

*Every minute, gravity pulls about 45 million gallons (170 million liters) of water over the cliffs at Niagara Falls.*

The "pulling" a person experiences on a roller coaster feels very much like the force of gravity's pull, so it was given the name g-force. Earth's gravity creates a g-force of 1 at sea level. At 1 g, things are their normal, expected weight. At 2 g, objects feel twice as heavy. If you were traveling in a spaceship where there was 0 g, you would feel completely weightless. Without gravity's pull, you would simply float around inside the cabin of the ship.

## GRAVITY AND ACCELERATION

Scientists have discovered that Earth's gravity (1 g) pulls objects toward its surface at a rate of 32.2 feet (9.8 m) per second. This means that for every

## EVERYDAY G-FORCES

*You don't have to visit an amusement park or be a race car driver to experience g-forces. Most people encounter g-forces every day.*

| Event | G's |
|---|---|
| standing | 1 |
| normal elevator acceleration (up) | 1.2 |
| commercial airliner during takeoff | 1.5 |
| walking down stairs | 1.5–2 |
| sneeze | 2.9 |
| cough | 3.5 |
| slap on the back | 4.1 |
| sitting down quickly in a chair | 10.1 |

Source: http://sportsillustrated.cnn.com/motorsports/news/2001/04/29/cart_cancel_ap/#more

second an object is falling, its speed will increase by 32.2 feet per second.

For example, imagine you dropped a coin from the top of a tall building into a fountain below. The speed of the coin is 0 feet per second when it first leaves your hand. After 1 second the coin would be traveling at 32.2 feet per second. Two seconds after the coin is dropped, it would be traveling at 64.4 feet (19.6 m) per second. The longer the coin falls, the faster it would go until it reaches its terminal, or maximum, velocity because of the resistance caused by the friction of the atmosphere. Gravity causes the coin, or any falling object, to accelerate over time. And acceleration causes g-force.

### SAME G-NUMBER, DIFFERENT IMPACT

The impact a particular g-force has on a person depends on the number

*Sneezes can be very forceful. Air moving from a person during a sneeze can reach speeds of 100 miles (160 km) per hour.*

of g's and the direction the g-force is applied, as well as how long it lasts. For example, a sneeze is a 2.9-g event that lasts a very short time—less than a second. A person who sneezes does not usually feel any major effects of this nearly 3-g event, where the head generally moves forward in one direction.

Now think about the intense feelings a rider on a roller coaster experiences while zipping up and down a high incline. This 3-g event lasts much longer, varies in direction as the coaster moves, and therefore causes significant feelings of pressure and exhilaration. A split-second g-force on one part of the body feels very different from a longer g-force on an entire body. The same g-force can have a very different impact on a person depending on how long it lasts.

# FOR THE ADVENTUROUS, AN EARTHBOUND RIDE ON THE SHUTTLE

*The New York Times*
June 8, 2007

Hitching a ride on the space shuttle comes to the lucky few only after a long selection process and arduous training. But the Kennedy Space Center visitor complex has worked with current and former astronauts to develop a ride that just may be the next best thing. …

At "liftoff" there are more sounds and shaking seats. The entire simulator rears back on hydraulic lifts, setting the passengers up at a nearly 70-degree angle. As the sound and shaking intensifies, air bladders concealed in the seat cushions soften to give the feeling of being pressed back into the seats by the three-G force of ascent.

Many kids think about becoming an astronaut when they grow up. They dream of blasting off into space and exploring new frontiers. But becoming an astronaut is not easy. Few people pass the intense tests and training required to become a space traveler.

The Kennedy Space Center created the Shuttle Launch Experience for visitors to experience the g's of a rocket blastoff. To help fulfill the dreams of many, the Kennedy Space Center built

*Former astronauts took part in one of the first simulations of the Shuttle Launch Experience when it opened in 2007.*

## NOW YOU KNOW

Ordinary people may be able to fly in space in the near future by purchasing a ticket for a ride on a spaceliner. Several spaceliner companies are currently selling seats on future space flights for $100,000 to $300,000.

four launch simulators. Each holds 44 people. Passengers on the Shuttle Launch Experience enjoy an exhilarating ride filled with realistic special effects created by astronauts and a technical design team. During this five-minute ride, the launch simulator shakes, jolts, and rocks backward. The simulation of powerful g-forces plays a major role in the realistic blastoff. Deflating seats help create the feeling of 3 g's that press down on astronauts as they hurtle toward space. At the end of the ride, large cargo bay doors open to reveal a beautiful image of Earth on a screen.

## GOING UP: POSITIVE G-FORCE

When real astronauts blast off for space, they are moving in the opposite direction of gravity's pull. This upward movement multiplies the effect of gravity and creates a powerful g-force that pushes astronauts firmly down into their seats. Accelerating away from the force of gravity creates a positive g-force. Positive g's make things feel heavier than they really are. The powerful positive g's during a blastoff make even the simplest movement—such as lifting an arm—very difficult.

Have you ever wondered how many g's an astronaut must handle during a real blastoff? Astronaut Koichi Wakata shares his real-life experiences with g-force during a rocket launch:

*At launch the gravity that we experience is about 1.7 g's and by the time the solid rocket boosters are separated, which is two minutes into the launch, the g-force will be over 2 g's. At the separation of the solid rocket booster, the g-force will decrease to just over 1 g. During the last one minute of the ascent, which is for 8.5 minutes, when the main engines ignited the last full minute, we will experience about 3 g's, and when the main engines cut off around 8 minutes, 30 seconds, you go right into zero-g and everything starts to float around.*

## WEIGHTLESSNESS

Once in space, astronauts find themselves in a zero-g environment. Far from the pull of Earth's gravity, they experience total weightlessness. Astronauts float around in their rocket ship, bouncing off of the walls and ceiling. With zero gravity, there is no force to keep things in their place.

*The Space Shuttle Discovery blasted off from the Kennedy Space Center in May 2008 on a mission to the International Space Station.*

*Crew members from the International Space Station posed for a weightless photo on Christmas in 2007.*

On Earth, gravity keeps a drink inside its cup. In space, drinks would float around in the cabin, so they are kept in pouches and sipped through a straw. To stay in bed at night, astronauts must zip themselves into sleeping bags that are attached to the wall.

## COMING DOWN: NEGATIVE G-FORCE

Just as positive g-forces are created when a person accelerates away from gravity's pull, negative g-forces occur when you move downward with gravity. Negative g-force provides a floating feeling. If you've ever ridden on a roller coaster, you may have experienced temporary weightlessness as you swooshed down a steep hill. You may have also experienced negative g's if you've been on an airplane that suddenly dropped in the air. When you move in the same direction as gravity, you feel as if you are floating.

# FLIGHT SCHOOL: AN ASSIGNMENT YOU CAN'T REFUSE

Jeffrey Kofman,
ABC News
February 16, 2008

I was at peace with the idea of my first ride on a fighter jet. Actually, I was a little excited ... until the public affairs officer at Eglin Air Force Base casually mentioned over the phone that as long as I liked roller coasters I'd have no problem in an F-16.

I hate roller coasters.

Yet there I was one recent Monday morning at the Medical Center at Eglin Air Force Base, near Pensacola, Fla., perched on the end of an examining bed as my ears and throat were probed by flight surgeon Maj. Bob Mishra. ...

"More than half the people get sick," [Mishra] told me in a disarmingly clinical voice. "Just make sure you get a couple of airsickness bags."

Like many people, Jeffrey Kofman was excited about the idea of riding in an F-16 fighter jet. But his initial excitement soon turned to fear when he learned about the unpleasant difficulties he might experience on the flight. Along with nausea and vomiting, Kofman was also told he might pass out. The g's during flight would push blood from Kofman's head into his legs, and the reduced blood supply to his brain could result in loss of consciousness.

As Kofman continued his pre-flight training, he discovered the cause of these side-effects. "Then I learned that

*Along with wearing a special suit that helps reduce the high g's encountered during flight, F-16 pilots wear oxygen masks because the air is thin (has less oxygen) at higher altitudes.*

the real demon in all this is gravitational force, or as they like to call it here, G force," he said.

After completing the training, Kofman decided he didn't want to miss the ride of his life, so he went ahead with the flight. The next morning Kofman woke at 4 A.M. and put on his flight suit. Following the advice of experienced pilots, he ate a light breakfast consisting of a few crackers.

Kofman and his pilot, nicknamed "Thunder," took to the sky shortly after 7 A.M. Once in flight Kofman kept his eyes on the horizon, a trick he learned during training to keep from getting airsick. Soaring across the blue sky, he marveled at the spectacular view from his seat on top of the plane. Feeling much better than he'd expected, his fear of g-forces soon subsided. But that didn't last for long. As Thunder banked the F-16 to the left, Kofman felt the incredible grip of g-force. He explained:

> *Suddenly I was overcome with a sensation unlike anything I'd felt before. It was as if King Kong had me in the palm of his hairy hand and he was trying to squeeze every ounce of blood out of me.*

Although Kofman felt good at the beginning of the flight, the 3 g's he later encountered during his first big turn was intense. As he continued to be affected by g-force, he eventually used several "barf bags." Near the end of the flight, the pilot asked Kofman if he wanted to try 6 g's before they headed in. Recalling the fearsome grip he experienced at 3 g's, Kofman promptly responded, "I think I'm good for today."

**NOW YOU KNOW**

Fighter jet pilots receive special training to withstand the high g-forces they face during flight. Most fighter pilots can tolerate up to 9 g's for a short time.

## G-FORCES PACK A PUNCH

Most people can withstand the small, short-term g-forces created during ordinary activities—such as sneezing, coughing, jumping, and running. Longer events with higher accelerations, such as riding in cars and airplanes and on amusement park rides, often create a g-force that can have big effects on people. G-force has been known to cause problems such as nausea, vertigo, dizziness, disorientation, reduced or lost vision, loss of consciousness, and hearing loss, as well as broken bones and burst blood vessels.

About 60 percent of your body weight is water, so it is not surprising that the squishy, water-filled human body is greatly affected by g-force. Even the outside of your body is covered by a thin, flexible tissue: skin. Although your body contains hard bones, it is mostly made of soft organs, such as the stomach, heart, kidneys, liver, lungs, and intestines, which are all loosely connected. Even the delicate brain can slide and move inside your skull. Body organs are easily shifted by g-force, and this movement can cause extreme discomfort.

Every person's body is different, and each person reacts to g-force in a different way. A human body can absorb a certain amount of g-forces, but when that unknown limit is reached, negative side-effects and injuries can result. Even those who are accustomed to high-g conditions—such as race car drivers—sometimes face g-forces that are too high and unsafe for them. According to *Sports Illustrated*, race car drivers came across this problem during an April 2001 race at Texas Motor Speedway. A particularly steep stretch of the track was affecting most of the drivers:

> *CART [Championship Auto Racing Teams] drivers refused to compete ... at Texas Motor Speedway over safety issues, saying G forces almost twice as high as normal were causing vision and hearing problems. ... "The G forces were beyond what I could have ever imagined," said Michael Andretti, the biggest winner in CART history.*

*Michael Andretti, winner of 38 CART races during his career, was inducted into the Motorsports Hall of Fame in 2008.*

Race cars drivers and other high-speed competitors realize that high g's can cause them to have impaired vision, loss of hearing, and other problems that may lead to needless accidents. They know when they encounter g-forces they can't handle, and they also know safety is very important.

## STUDYING G-FORCE

To help people involved in high-g activities stay safe, some scientists today are studying g-forces and how they affect people. These "g-force specialists" use accelerometers to measure g-force levels. An accelerometer is an instrument that measures the strength and length of g-forces created during an impact. There are many types of accelerometers, but most are small and thin. Scientists who collect g-force data often use accelerometers smaller than a dime for their testing. These tiny instruments can easily be placed inside a helmet or other location on the test subject.

Human tolerance to g-force depends on several factors, such as the g-force magnitude, how long the g-force is applied, and the direction the g-force is applied. Where the g-force is applied on a person's body and the body position also determine the effect of the g-force.

People who must work in high-g conditions, such as pilots and astronauts, go through special g-force training. During training they are exposed to g-forces above 1 g so they can get used to it and practice various techniques that are known to reduce g-force side-effects. These techniques include various body positions, tightening of leg and abdominal muscles, and breathing exercises. Through experimentation, trainees decide which techniques work best for them. Then they practice various techniques and learn the best way to

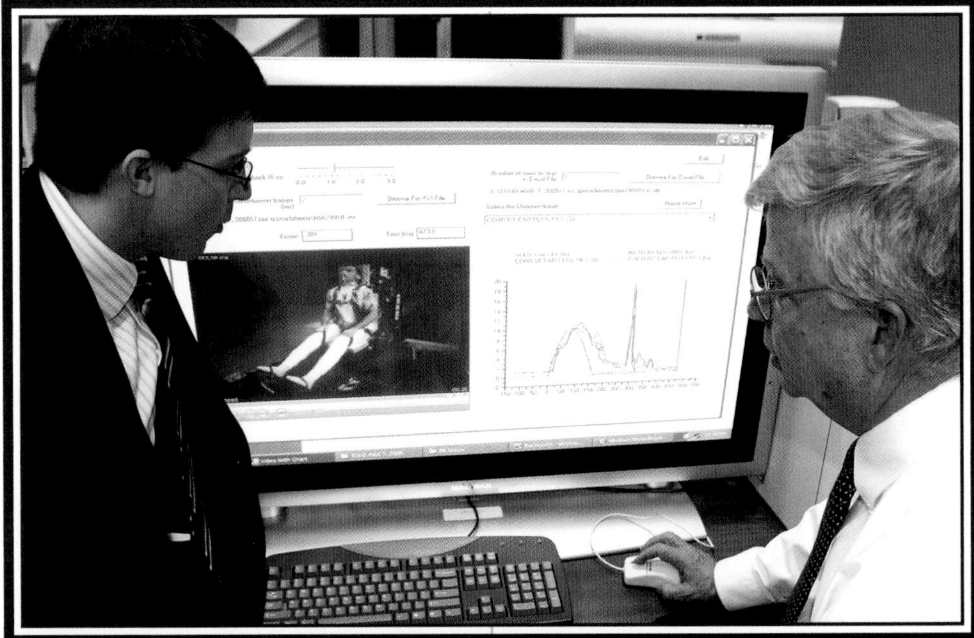

*Joseph Pellettiere (left) and Ted Knox of the Air Force Research Laboratory near Dayton, Ohio, reviewed data and video feeds from an accelerator test. The accelerators measured the speed of a driver's head during various levels of impact.*

*Before opening to the public, Wicked Twister, a ride at Cedar Point in Sandusky, Ohio, was tested using water-filled dummies. The test showed the effects the wild ride would have on its passengers.*

execute each one in order to combat the negative effects of high g's.

F-16 pilot Lieutenant Colonel Rob Skelton regularly faces 9 g's, but his extensive training helps him to handle these high g-forces with ease:

> *Thursday was a typical day for Air Force Lt. Col. Rob Skelton as he steered his F-16 fighter jet in a tight turn at 600 mph [960 km/h] above the Charlotte County Airport. The maneuver was so sharp that the force upon the jet reached 9.2 Gs, enough to make most people black out for a second. But Skelton's training, and the training for all Air Force F-16 pilots, allowed him to maintain complete control.*

# A LIGHT AT THE END OF THE HALF-PIPE, THROUGH CLOSED EYES

Harry Hurt III
*The New York Times*
January 26, 2008

The last thing I saw before plunging down the bobsled track at the Olympic Sports Complex outside Lake Placid, N.Y., was an eerie orange light. ... I realized that the orange light was the sunset reflecting off the summit of Whiteface Mountain a dozen or so miles to the north. But I had no idea whether it foreboded the thrill of a lifetime or imminent death. ...

Next thing I knew, we lurched forward and downward. ... Suddenly, I felt a crushing G-force. ... At what I later learned was Turn 15, the start of the heart-shaped section of the track, I felt the sled slow and the G-forces drop. For an instant, I thought—make that, hoped—that the ride was over. Instead, we picked up speed again.

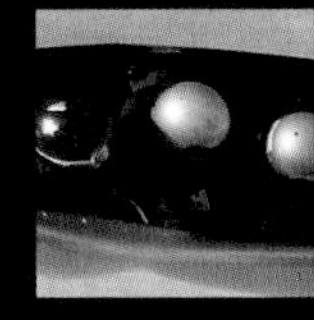

Seated in the third seat of a four-man bobsled, reporter Harry Hurt III felt the incredible crushing power of g-force as he hurtled down the Lake Placid bobsled track on a 14-foot (4.3-m) fiberglass sled. With its four passengers, the sled weighed more than 1,400 pounds (635 kg). The bobsled reached a top speed of 72 miles (116 km) per hour during its 52-second journey down the ¾-mile (1.2-km) track. On his first-ever bobsled ride, Hurt survived 20 nail-biting turns and a vertical drop equal to a 40-story building. During his short and treacherous trip, he quickly learned what most athletes in high-speed or impact sports already know. "As I soon discovered, gravity could be either friend or foe," Hurt said.

*During fall and winter, the Olympic Sports Complex in Lake Placid, New York, offers people the chance to experience high g's during a ride on its famous bobsled or luge tracks.*

## COMBINING VARIOUS TYPES OF ACCELERATION

The g-forces Hurt experienced on his bobsled ride were powerful because various types of acceleration combined as he sped down the icy hill. The bobsled gained speed, or accelerated, in the straight sections of the track. It changed direction suddenly at each turn, which created another type of acceleration. This combination had some serious effects on the unsuspecting bobsled novice. Forceful g-forces pressed and pulled on Hurt as he careened around sharp curves.

"The bobsled dove to the left. My head pressed down on my neck. My stomach leaped up into my throat," Hurt explained. At times he experienced 4 g's pushing down on his body. "Before I could exhale a grateful breath, the sled jerked back to the right, yanking my torso sideways until it was parallel to the floor of the track. My shoulders collapsed under pressure equal to four times the pull of gravity."

*Motocross racers must frequently accelerate, decelerate, and change directions around a winding motocross track.*

## G'S IN THE CURVE

There are many sports in which athletes encounter curves, which cause acceleration that is due to a changing direction. Motocross racers, race car drivers, and speed skaters experience high g's from acceleration caused by changing direction, slowing down, and speeding up. Downhill skiers also face sharp curves as they maneuver around flags and over jumps. To stay in control and reduce the effects of high g's, most athletes slow down before entering a turn.

Have you ever ridden on a spinning ride at an amusement park? If so, you've experienced the strong g-force these revolving rides create. One attraction called the Gravitron holds its passengers against the wall, while the floor below completely

*Spinning rides at amusement parks use g-forces. The rapid spinning motion pushes the passengers outward and pins them to the cushions along the side of the ride.*

drops away. As the riders spin, the power of 3 g's pins them to the outside wall. But what causes those amazing g's that are able to attach people to the curved outer wall? The answer is acceleration. The passengers on this ride are always changing direction, which is a form of acceleration, as they constantly move around in a circle.

## ASTRONAUT TESTING

NASA uses a spinning piece of equipment called a centrifuge to help astronauts train for the 3 g's they will encounter during blastoff and the

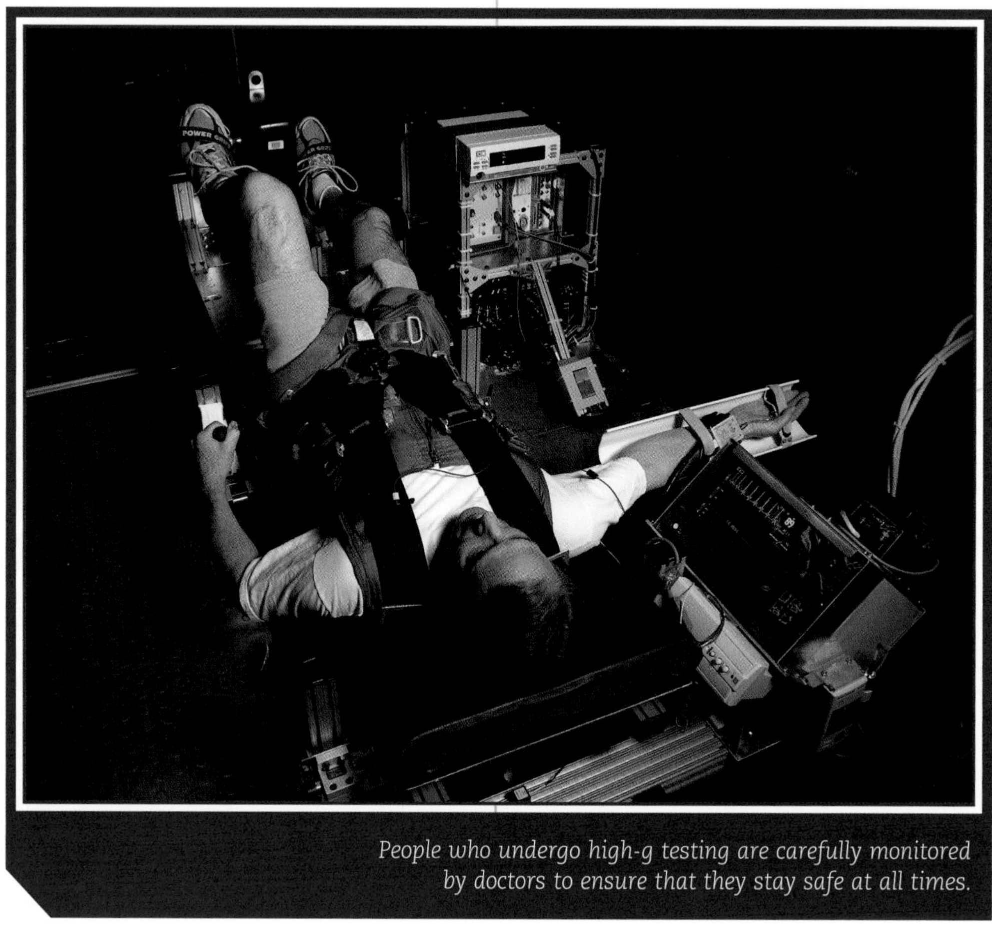

*People who undergo high-g testing are carefully monitored by doctors to ensure that they stay safe at all times.*

## LEARNING TO COPE WITH

NASA's largest g-force testing facility is located in California at the Ames Research Center. The human centrifuge at Ames can create forces up to 20 g's. The research experiments conducted in the 20-g centrifuge help scientists learn new ways astronauts can more easily cope with the lower g's during flight, and how they can adjust to Earth's gravity when returning home.

approximate 1.4-g re-entry. A centrifuge has a small cabin, or cell, on the end of a long arm. As the arm of the centrifuge spins, the astronaut inside the cell experiences higher than normal g-forces. This exposure to hypergravity, or g-forces above 1 g, helps astronauts prepare for space flight. Some astronauts ride in a centrifuge for a short time, such as a few hours, while others may be required to stay inside for longer training sessions lasting several weeks.

### TRY IT YOURSELF

You could try a simple experiment at home to help you understand spinning objects and g-force. To begin, tie a small ball or rock on the end of a piece of string. Then hold the other end of the string tightly as you spin the object tied to it. As it moves, you will feel the string pulling on your hand. Try to keep the object spinning at the same speed so you can experience the pulling sensation created only by the change of direction.

# AFL TO TEST DEVICE TO WARN OF POSSIBLE CONCUSSIONS

*Orlando Sentinel*
March 6, 2008

Orlando Predators quarterback Shane Stafford knows every player in the Arena Football League will suffer a hit that will make him woozy. ...

The AFL is hoping a new device being tested during games this season will help team trainers, doctors, coaches and players understand when to take the big hits seriously and calm growing concerns about concussions in all levels of football.

The device, tentatively dubbed the "Shockometer" by manufacturer Schutt Sports, is shaped like a triangle. The 2-inch meter has an adhesive that sticks to the back of helmets. When a player is hit by a G-force in excess of 98 to 100, a capsule with green fluid turns red.

Football players, as well as athletes in other sports, can be injured by g-forces from hard hits during a game. Athletes in contact sports try to protect themselves from harmful hits with pads and helmets. In recent years, scientists have begun developing new technologies for people in high g-force activities.

The shockometer is a new safety device some football teams are testing on their players. This small, thin triangle gets its name from the quick acceleration, called shock, caused by a sudden hit. Doctors believe hits that create more than 100 g may cause concussions. It's difficult for coaches and trainers to know which hits are above that dangerous number. Using a device that can measure g-force helps players and doctors know when a player might be seriously injured.

*The intense hits and tackles during AFL games caused concern for the players' safety.*

"It sounds like a very simple concept, but we were looking for a way to take some of the guessing out of how to treat players with head injuries quickly," said Dave Rossi, chief marketing officer for Schutt Sports. "If you see the red light, you know it's time to examine the player more closely."

While this tiny capsule on a football player's helmet won't lessen g-forces on the field, it does give the team's staff crucial information about the hit an injured player receives and helps support personnel make important decisions for treatment.

## THE RIGHT GEAR

Football is just one of many rough contact sports. Athletes who participate in soccer, football, hockey, lacrosse, baseball, and other sports often experience sudden impacts that create a temporary—but powerful—g-force. To help protect against sudden g's, many players wear certain kinds of pads, specially designed guards, and helmets. Many wear mouth guards to protect their teeth from hard impacts. Baseball catchers use chest protectors to absorb the g's of fast, incoming pitches. Wearing the proper gear helps

*Lacrosse players use several pieces of protective equipment, including a helmet, shoulder pads, arm pads, gloves, and sometimes even rib pads.*

keep athletes safe, so make sure you put on your safety gear before heading out to play.

Even if you're not involved in a high-impact sport, you should still protect yourself while doing activities where you might fall. Seemingly simple falls create quick g's that may cause serious injuries, such as broken bones and concussions. Always wear a helmet and appropriate safety gear when biking, inline skating, skateboarding, or snowboarding. Put on your seat belt every time you ride in the car. You never know when you will be in an accident. The right safety equipment will keep you safe from dangerous g-forces.

*U.S. Navy Captain Dan Doorman puts on his g-suit before taking part in flying exercises at Elmendorf Air Force Base in Alaska.*

## G-SUITS

People such as pilots and astronauts who participate in extremely high-g activities need more than helmets and pads. These high fliers face g-force levels that can cause g-induced loss of consciousness (g-LOC), or blackouts. This serious side-effect occurs when blood pools in the lower part of the body because of the pressure of g-force. The excessive blood collecting in the legs causes a lack of blood—and therefore oxygen—in the brain. To keep a sufficient flow of blood to the brain, those who take to the skies wear a special piece of equipment called an antigravity suit, or g-suit.

Pilots usually go through several "warning" stages before g-LOC. The first stage, called a brownout, begins when high g-forces cause blood to move to the lower part of the body. This pooling of blood in the lower body creates a reduced flow of blood, and therefore oxygen, to the head. During a brownout, vision becomes dim or blurry because of the lower oxygen supply. In the next stage, people experience tunnel-vision, which is a condition in which people are only able to see things directly in front of them. This condition is caused by a lesser blood flow—and therefore oxygen—to the eyes. In the final stage, also known as blackout, there is a complete loss of consciousness or g-LOC. This is caused by less oxygen and a weak blood flow to the brain.

*Normal vision*

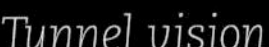

*Tunnel vision*

First developed in 1940, g-suits are basically a tight-fitting pair of pants with inflatable bladders. When a pilot or astronaut experiences high g-force levels during flight, the bladders are activated, or inflated. These bladders press on the abdomen and legs of the wearer, keeping excess blood from leaving the head during periods of high-g's or acceleration.

There are several kinds of g-suits. Some use pressurized air to inflate the bladders, while others are filled with liquid. Pilots who fly airplanes that create very high g's wear g-suits that provide a small amount of pressure to the lungs, in addition to the bladders that press on the abdomen and legs. This additional pressure on the lungs helps them breathe easier. Some antigravity suits are full-body g-suits. They cover most of the body, including the hands.

# SALVAGE JOB: JEFF GORDON'S SEASON IS ON THE LINE IN MICHIGAN

Lars Anderson
*Sports Illustrated*
June 16, 2006

It's the driver's worst-case scenario: Roaring down a straightaway at top speed and having your brakes go out. Put simply, it's the downright scariest thing in motor sports.

So there was Jeff Gordon last Sunday at Pocono Raceway. Late in the Pocono 500, his No. 24 DuPont Chevy flew around Turn 4 and Gordon mashed the gas. ... Then, as he closed in on Turn 1, it happened: Gordon hit the brakes and ... nothing. ...

Gordon then slid onto the track and bashed into the wall in what had to be the hardest, most violent lick I've seen in my three years on the NASCAR beat. Amazingly, Gordon crawled out of his car, unhurt.

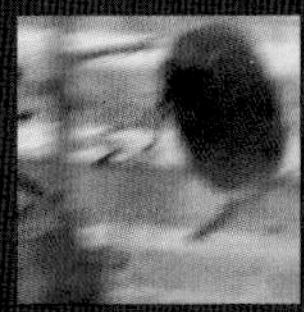

When Jeff Gordon's race car hit the outside barrier wall at 200 miles (320 km) per hour, 100,000 fans in the grandstand silently watched the cockpit for any sign of movement. When Gordon's voice finally crackled over his car radio, the crowd let out a collective sigh of relief.

"That was one of the hardest hits I have ever taken," Gordon said. "Between the soft wall and the seat and the safety device, I never got knocked out and I was surprised that I feel pretty good." Doctors who treated Gordon immediately after he climbed out of his car were surprised, too—especially after they learned Gordon's crash registered 64 g.

People who experience dangerously high g-forces usually do so by

*With 10 laps left in the 2006 Pocono 500, Jeff Gordon's car experienced a brake failure during the longest straightaway of the course.*

**Race car driver Kenny Brack survived one of the highest g-force events in history. He crashed his car during a race at the Texas Indy 500 in 2003. With just 10 laps to go, Brack's car came in contact with another vehicle, causing his car to fly through the air and hit a large steel pole in the fence. That sudden deceleration created an enormous g-force. Some believed it was a whopping 214 g! Although Brack suffered broken bones and injuries that kept him in the hospital for about a year, he eventually recovered from his record g-force crash.**

accident. Many survive, but some do not. Knowing the risks involved, it's hard to imagine anyone would choose to be in such a crash on purpose. But one man did just that. John Stapp voluntarily took part in test crashes and set many g-force records—all in the pursuit of safety.

## G-FORCE CRASH TESTING

It all began in 1945 when the U.S. War Department started a new project to make flying safer for its pilots. Colonel John Stapp, a doctor in the military, was assigned to analyze g-force data from plane crashes for this project. At that time, engineers and plane designers believed people could survive a maximum of 18 g, so the plane's cockpit and safety equipment were designed to withstand that g-force. Stapp began to question this "magic" number when he found data on pilots who died in crashes below 18 g, while others had survived crashes over 18 g. He concluded the seats, harnesses, and cockpits had failed during many of these crashes, and that they were the real source of death. Stapp soon realized pilot fatalities could be reduced if more was known about the body's ability to withstand certain g-forces, or human g-force tolerance. Then airplane safety equipment could be designed around that information.

Stapp and his research team decided to conduct crash tests to determine human g-force tolerance to sudden stops, or deceleration. By gathering this information, they hoped to discover how to better protect people from high g's. To begin, Stapp's

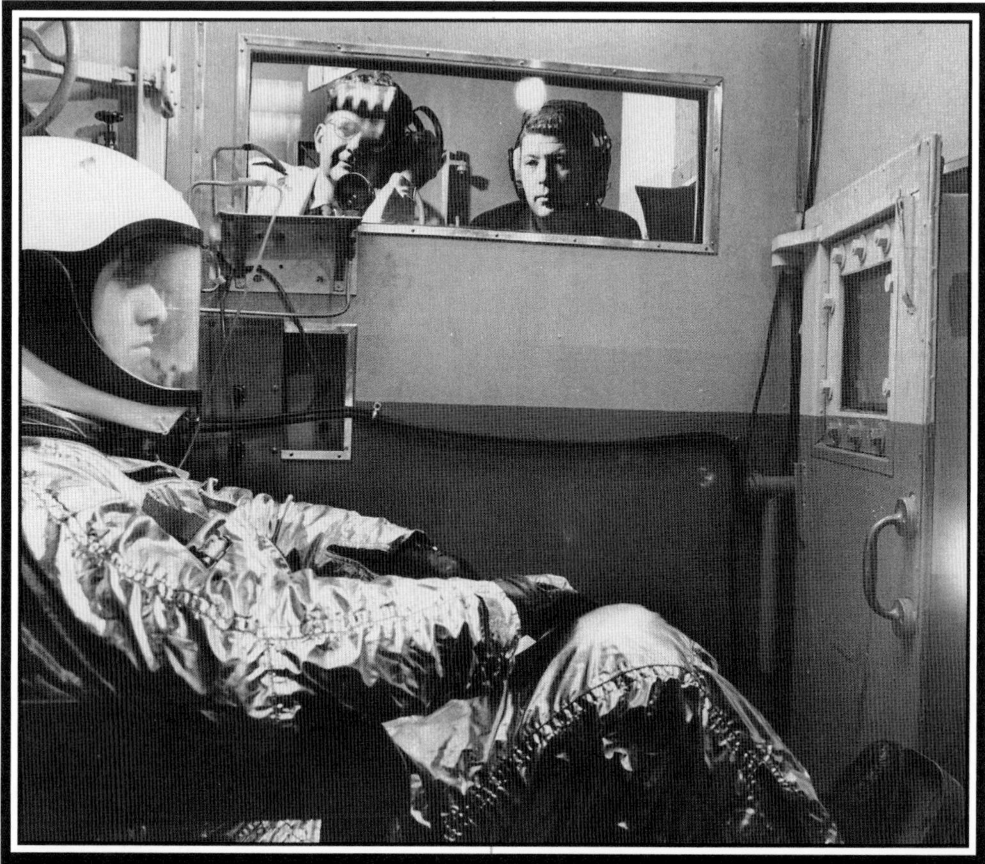

*John Stapp (left rear) watched a test through the window of the Altitude Chamber—a room that simulates high altitudes and records the effects it has on the human body.*

team built a 1,500-pound (680-kg) sled named Gee Whiz from welded tubes. They attached rockets on the back for powerful acceleration. The sled was also equipped with hydraulic brakes for a quick stop. Runners were installed on the bottom of Gee Whiz so it could easily glide across the 2,000 feet (610 m) of railroad test track. Finally, the sled was ready for its passenger Oscar Eightball, a 185-pound (84-kg) test dummy.

On Oscar's first test run, the rocket sled accelerated to 150 miles (241 km) per hour before the powerful brakes were applied. The resulting 30 g's broke the seat belt, and Oscar landed more than 700 feet (213 m) from the rocket. For each of the 30 test runs that followed, valuable test data were recorded, and the rocket's safety equipment was tweaked and redesigned.

**NOW YOU KNOW**

"Eyeballs in" is the phrase used to describe the pushing-back feeling caused by g-force when a person accelerates forward in a straight line. "Eyeballs out" is the phrase that describes the forward, pulling sensation a person feels from g-force when decelerating in a straight line.

## THE HUMAN DECELERATOR

After eight months of collecting data, Colonel Stapp decided it was time to learn how high g-force impacts would affect a real person. Although these tolerance tests were dangerous, he willingly volunteered to ride the rocket sled and become a "human decelerator." In 1947, Stapp passed his first test run of 10 g's with flying colors. Afterward, he commented that the ride was "quite pleasant."

On the 15 tests that followed, Stapp was exposed to higher and higher g-forces. Eventually he survived an 18-g run, proving this g-force did not mean certain death. He later endured an unbelievable 35 g! Although Stapp was pleased with his

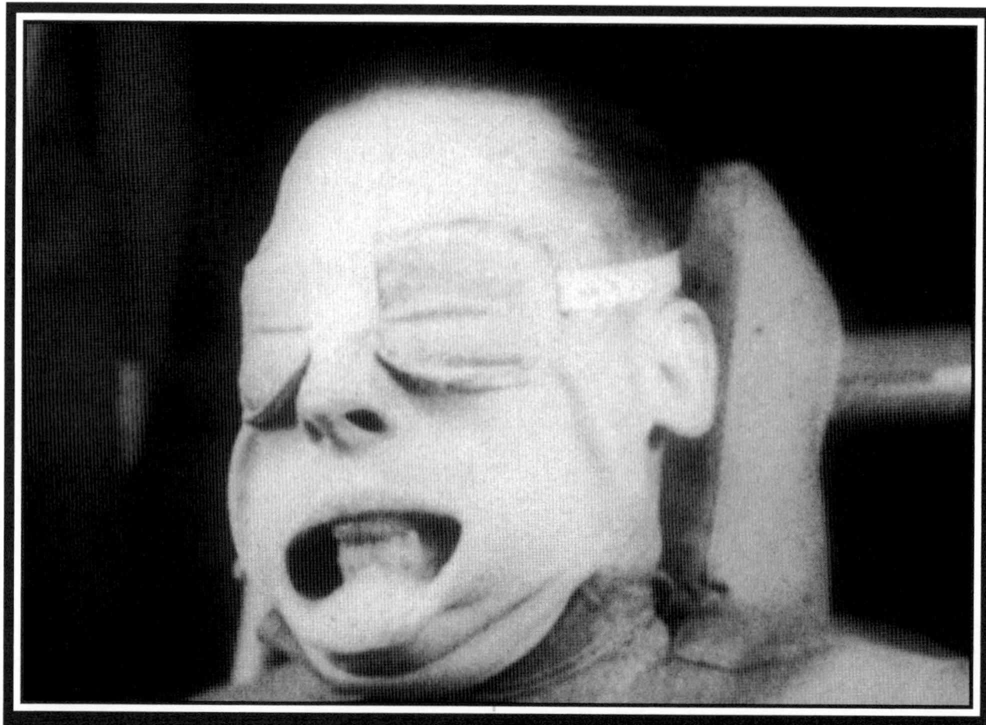

*As part of the safety precautions, a test subject wore padded eye protection and sat in a heavily cushioned chair during intense g-force testing.*

discoveries about human g-force tolerance, his research came with a price. Because of the powerful g's he experienced, Stapp ended up with concussions, cracked ribs, and broken wrists. He also broke blood vessels in his eyes and lost fillings in his teeth. But Stapp's hard work and sacrifice paid off. The Air Force realized pilots could survive a 30-g crash. They decided to redesign their seats, harnesses, and cockpits to withstand 30 g as well. These new safety features saved countless future pilots from needless injuries and even death.

## FASTEST MAN ON EARTH

Although John Stapp accomplished a great deal during his test runs on Gee Whiz, he wasn't done with

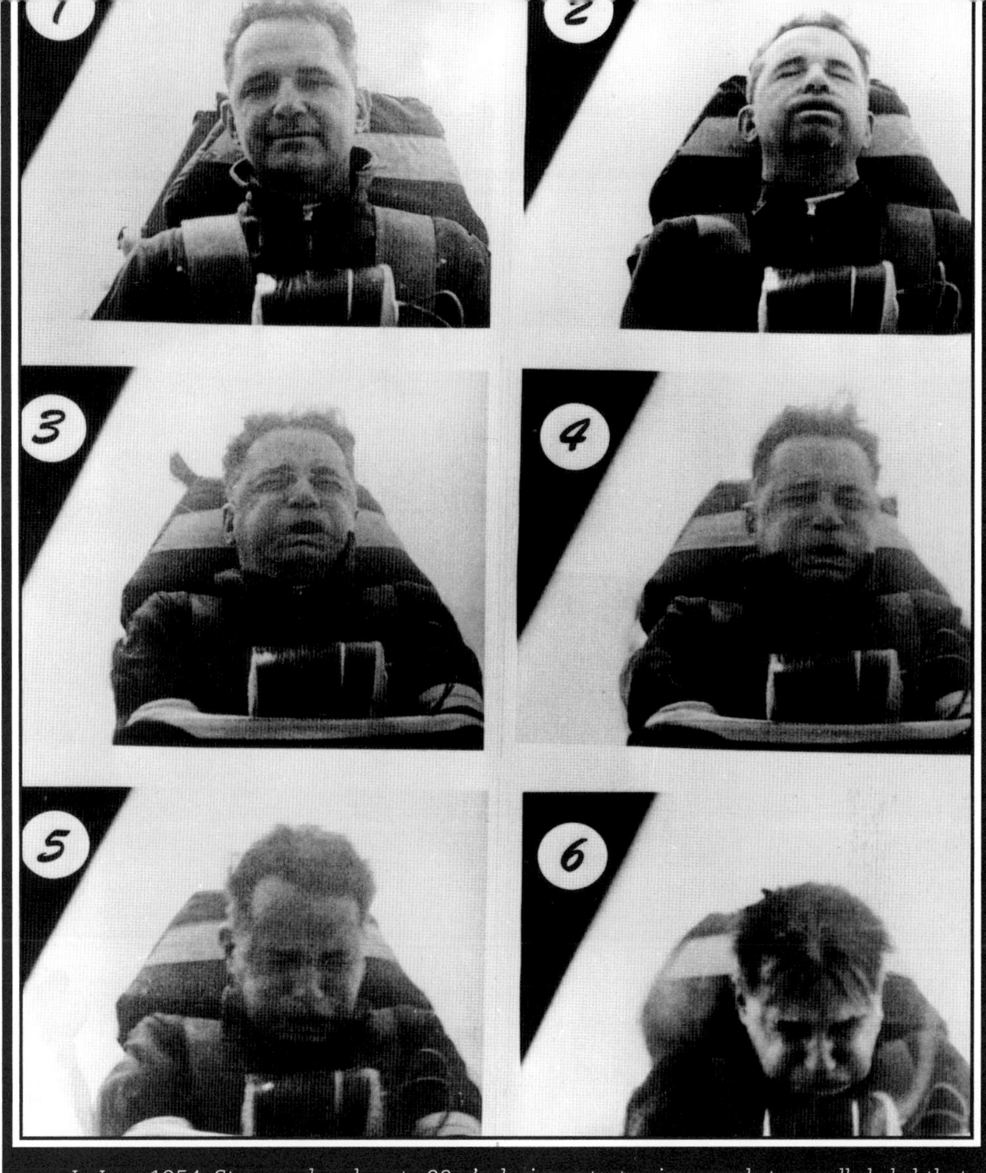


*In June 1954, Stapp endured up to 22 g's during a test using a rocket-propelled sled that reached more than 400 miles (640 km) per hour. Pictures 1–3 show the first five seconds of the acceleration, and pictures 4–6 show Stapp's reaction to the instant deceleration.*



g-force testing yet. In 1954, he took his 29th—and last—test ride on a new sled called Sonic Wind. The sled was equipped with nine rockets and accelerated to a speed of 632 miles (1,011 km) per hour in seconds. While at this top speed, the water brakes were applied, and Stapp stopped in

*In celebration of the 50th anniversary of John Stapp's 1954 test, the Sonic Wind rocket sled re-enacted Stapp's legendary run on December 10, 2004.*

only 1.4 seconds. This rapid deceleration subjected him to a record 46.2 g! Remarkably, Stapp survived, but his eyes filled with blood during the stop, and he was blinded for about a day. After that famous ride, Stapp became known as the fastest man on Earth.

Stapp's research not only made planes safer, but his g-force data helped prompt safety changes in cars as well. His work proved humans could withstand the high g's of most car crashes if they were properly restrained. With data in hand, Stapp lobbied the Detroit car manufacturers to install seat belts in cars, a safety device not offered at that time. For years he tried to persuade car makers to add other safety features, such as bumpers, softer dashboards, and collapsible steering wheels. Eventually they listened. By voluntarily subjecting

*Julie Nimmons, president of the Schutt Sports equipment company, displayed a new helmet that replaced traditional foam cushioning with shock-absorbing pads that are also used in the Army.*

himself to tremendous g-force tests, Colonel John Stapp made airplane and automobile travel safer for everyone.

## G-FORCE RESEARCH CONTINUES

G-forces are part of your everyday life. Each time you hop, sneeze, or cough, your body absorbs small, sudden g's. This mysterious force also provides exciting thrills on roller coaster and other rides, but it can be dangerous. Race car drivers, pilots, astronauts, and hard-hitting athletes must learn how to combat the negative effects of high g's.

Scientists are continuing to study human g-force tolerance. Their research has led to improved g-suits that allow pilots and astronauts to withstand higher g's than ever before. New advances in other g-force technologies, such as the shockometer for helmets, also help reduce injuries for athletes in high-impact sports. By understanding how the human body reacts to various g-force conditions, people are able to participate in many high-speed activities and still stay safe.

# Timeline

**1917**
The first cases are documented of pilots losing consciousness because of g-forces

**1940**
The first g-suit, which contained inflatable bladders for the legs and abdomen, is created by a team at the University of Toronto's Banting and Best Institute

**1941**
The first test centrifuge is built as a top-secret project in Canada; it effectively created g-forces similar to those in flight

**1942**
An early g-suit design, called the Franks Flying Suit Mark III, is worn in combat for the first time by pilots in the Royal Navy Fleet Air Arm

**1945**
The U.S. War Department studies the effects of g-force on people as part of a new aviation safety project

**1948**
Colonel John Stapp survives a test run of 18 g

**1954**
Stapp survives a record 46.2 g for several seconds on his rocket sled

**1954–1956**
Canadian Roy Stubbs develops the full-body pressure suit, or g-suit, at the Royal Air Force Institute of Aviation Medicine in Farnborough, England

**1977**
Formula One driver David Purley survives about 179 g when his car hits a wall and decelerates from 108 miles (173 km) per hour to 0

**2001**
CART race car drivers refuse to race at the Texas Motor Speedway on April 29 because of high-g conditions on the racetrack

**2003**
Race car driver Kenny Brack survives a high-speed crash that created a g-force of approximately 214 g

**2005**
The world's tallest and fastest roller coaster, Kingda Ka, opens at Six Flags Great Adventure in New Jersey, producing high-g thrills for riders

**2007**
NASA opens the Shuttle Launch Experience, a ride that simulates a 3-g rocket blastoff, at the Kennedy Space Center in Florida

**2008**
The Arena Football League begins testing shockometers on helmets to learn about the g-forces players encounter during a game

# GLOSSARY

**acceleration**
how fast an object speeds up, slows down, or changes direction

**accelerometer**
special device that measures the strength and length of g-forces created by an impact

**ascent**
process of moving upward

**bladder**
sack that holds gas or liquids

**centrifuge**
spinning device that creates high g-forces on the rider inside for testing and training purposes

**decelerate**
to reduce speed

**disorientation**
when a person feels confused or unsure of his or her location

**g-force**
measure of acceleration

**g-force tolerance**
human body's ability to withstand g-force

**g-induced loss of consciousness (g-LOC)**
loss of consciousness, or blackout, caused by high g's

**g-suit**
special suit worn by pilots and astronauts to help them combat the negative effects of higher g-forces during flight

**hydraulic brakes**
brake system that operates by using fluid pressure

**hypergravity**
g-forces measuring about 1 g

**negative g-force**
g-force created when an object moves downward in the same direction as the pull of gravity

**positive g-force**
g-force created when an object moves upward in the opposite direction of the pull of gravity

**terminal velocity**
the maximum velocity of a falling object limited by the friction between the object and the atmosphere

**vertigo**
feeling of dizziness or lightheadedness, often brought on from a fear of heights

# FURTHER RESOURCES

## ON THE WEB

For more information on this topic, use FactHound.

1. Go to *www.facthound.com*
2. Choose your grade level.
3. Begin your search.

This book's ID number is 9780756540524

FactHound will find the best sites for you.

## FURTHER READING

Cooper, Christopher. *Forces and Motion: From Push to Shove.* Chicago: Heinemann Library, 2003.

Hammond, Richard. *Can You Feel the Force?* New York: DK Publishing, 2006.

Nardo, Don. *Force and Motion.* Minneapolis: Compass Point Books, 2008.

Lepora, Nathan. *Falling for Fun: Gravity in Action.* Pleasantville, N.Y.: Gareth Stevens Publishing, 2008.

## LOOK FOR OTHER BOOKS IN THIS SERIES:

*Climate Crisis: The Science of Global Warming*

*Collapse!: The Science of Structural Engineering Failures*

*Cure Quest: The Science of Stem Cell Research*

*Goodbye, Gasoline: The Science of Fuel Cells*

*Great Shakes: The Science of Earthquakes*

*Orbiting Eyes: The Science of Artificial Satellites*

*Out of Control: The Science of Wildfires*

*Rise of the Thinking Machines: The Science of Robots*

*Storm Surge: The Science of Hurricanes*

# URCE NOTES


Chapter 1: Scott Frost. "Matchup of Man Vs. Machine: Rebel Reporter Slays Kingda Ka in Debut Run." *The Trentonian*. 20 May 2005. 13 Oct. 2008. www.zwire.com/site/news.cfm?newsid=14560165&BRD=1697&PAG=461&dept_id=44551&rfi=6

Chapter 2: John Schwartz. "For the Adventurous, an Earthbound Ride on the Shuttle." *The New York Times*. 8 June 2007. 13 Oct. 2008. www.nytimes.com/2007/06/08/science/space/08ride.html?scp=9&sq=g-force&st=nyt

Chapter 3: Jeffrey Kofman. "Flight School: An Assignment You Can't Refuse." ABC News. 16 Feb. 2008. 13 Oct. 2008. www.abcnews.go.com/Technology/story?id=3761623&page=1

Chapter 4: Harry Hurt III. "A Light at the End of the Half-pipe, Through Closed Eyes." *The New York Times*. 26 Jan. 2008. 13 Oct. 2008. www.nytimes.com/2008/01/26/business/smallbusiness/26pursuits.html?pagewanted=1&sq=g-force&st=nyt&scp=2

Chapter 5: Iliana Limon. "AFL to Test Device Designed to Warn of Possible Concussions." *Orlando Sentinel*. 6 March 2008. 13 Oct. 2008. www.orlandosentinel.com/sports/orl-arena0608mar06,0,5366928.story

Chapter 6: Lars Anderson. "Salvage Job: Jeff Gordon's Season is on the Line in Michigan." *Sports Illustrated*. 16 June 2006. 13 Oct. 2008. http://sportsillustrated.cnn.com/2006/writers/lars_anderson/06/16/jeff.gordon/


# ABOUT THE AUTHOR

Suzanne B. Slade is the author of more than 60 books for children and young adults. She holds an engineering degree and often writes about science topics. During her engineering career, she tested Delta IV rockets and designed automotive brake components. She currently writes from her home outside Chicago where she lives with her husband, Mike, and two children, Christina and Patrick.